Librarians at Work

by Karen Latchana Kenney
illustrated by Brian Caleb Dumm

Content Consultant:
Judith Stepan-Norris, PhD
Professor of Sociology, University of California, Irvine

Meet Your Community Workers!

magic
wagon

Published by Magic Wagon, a division of the ABDO Group, 8000 West 78th Street, Edina, Minnesota 55439. Copyright © 2010 by Abdo Consulting Group, Inc. International copyrights reserved in all countries. All rights reserved. No part of this book may be reproduced in any form without written permission from the publisher.

Looking Glass Library™ is a trademark and logo of Magic Wagon.

Printed in the United States.

 Manufactured with paper containing at least 10% post-consumer waste

Text by Karen Latchana Kenney
Illustrations by Brian Caleb Dumm
Edited by Patricia Stockland
Interior layout and design by Emily Love
Cover design by Emily Love

Library of Congress Cataloging-in-Publication Data
Kenney, Karen Latchana.
  Librarians at work / by Karen L. Kenney ; illustrated by Brian Caleb Dumm ; content consultant, Judith Stepan-Norris.
     p. cm. — (Meet your community workers)
  Includes index.
  ISBN 978-1-60270-649-1
  1. Librarians—Juvenile literature. 2. Library science—Vocational guidance—Juvenile literature. I. Dumm, Brian Caleb, ill. II. Title.
  Z682.K46 2010
  020.92—dc22
                       2009002386

Table of Contents

Being a Librarian

Are you looking for a certain book? Try asking a librarian. It is part of a librarian's job to help people find information. Librarians listen to questions. They decide what kind of information a person needs.

A person might need a book, magazine, journal, newspaper, CD, or DVD. They may also need to look on the Internet. Librarians find information and help people find things on their own. They also buy and prepare library materials. They sort the library materials into groups.

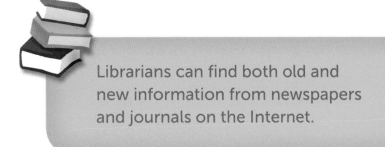

Librarians can find both old and new information from newspapers and journals on the Internet.

Helping Others

Librarians help many people. Students need information to help them study. In a school, a librarian helps a teacher. Some people who do not speak English might need help finding information. Some librarians work with children and young adults. Other librarians have special skills to help older adults.

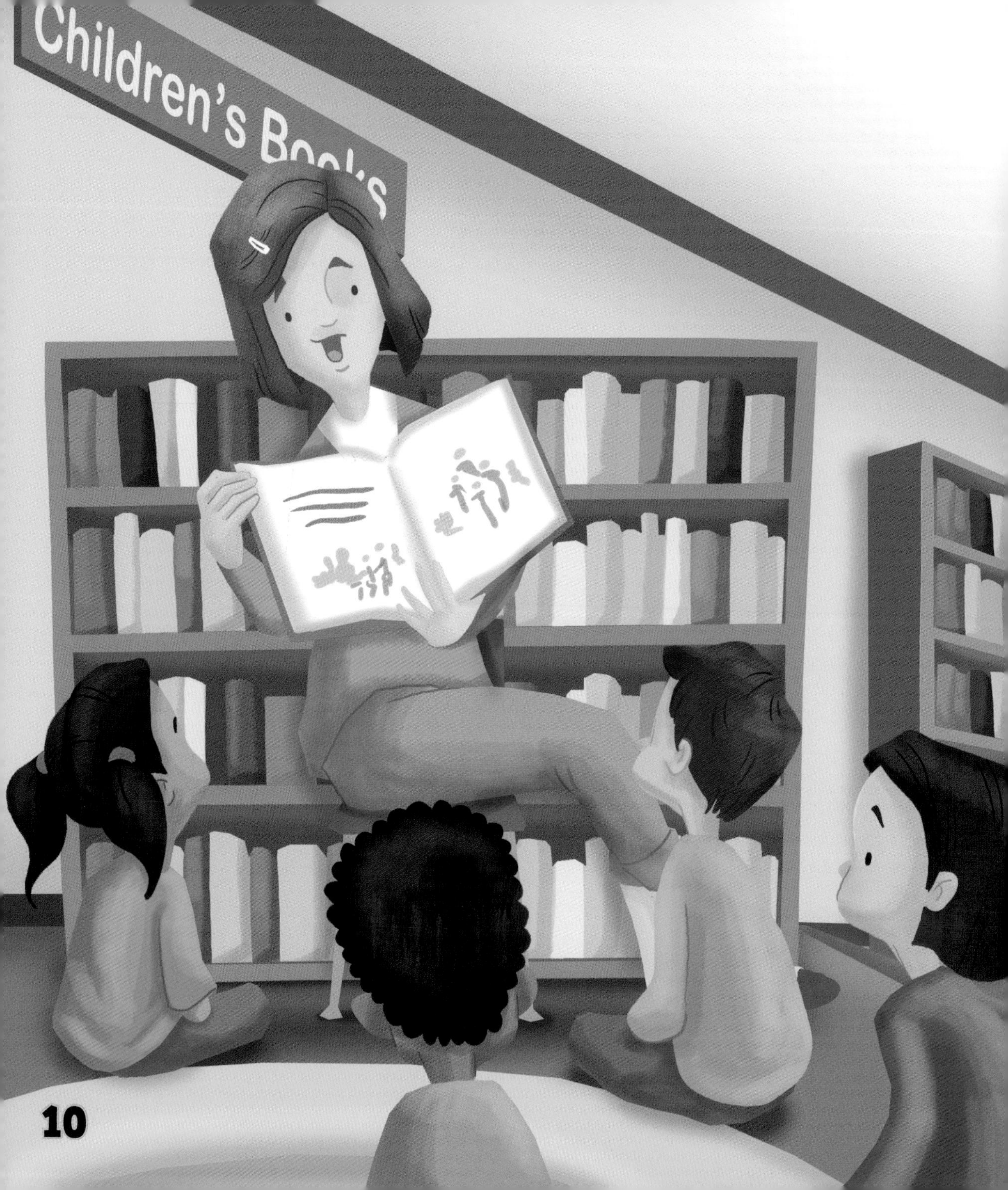
Children's Books

A librarian works with a team of people. People also volunteer to work at a library. Volunteers put books on shelves or help in other ways. Librarians direct these people.

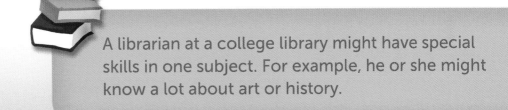

A librarian at a college library might have special skills in one subject. For example, he or she might know a lot about art or history.

Problems on the Job

It can be hard to help many people at the same time. Some people need information quickly. Librarians have to work fast. They must lift and carry books. Sometimes they climb ladders. Librarians might have to work at night or on the weekend. Sometimes they work on holidays.

Tools Librarians Need

A librarian's desk is in the middle of a library. This makes it easy to help people. Librarians read catalogs from places that make books. People rate these books. The rated books are listed in journals. Librarians look at catalogs and journals to find great books to buy.

Technology at Work

Computers are important tools for librarians. There are special computer programs used just at libraries. Some of these programs are called catalogs. They sort and store information about the materials in a library. This information is also on a library's Web site.

One big job for many librarians is digitizing books, journals, and newspapers. In this electronic format, information is easier to find.

Librarians use the Internet to find information. They use databases to find information that is not at their library. Web sites are on the Internet, too. Information on the Internet is not always correct, though. Librarians need to check information sources and know which are trustworthy.

Special Skills and Training

Librarians must have good listening skills. They also need to speak and write well. Librarians have to be able to figure out problems. Computer skills are necessary too. Librarians should also like to work with people.

LIBRARIAN
EXAM

To be a librarian, you first need to go to college. Then you need to study library skills. In some states, a person has to take a license test to be a librarian. Librarians also take classes to learn new skills. This helps them to be good at their jobs.

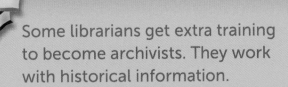

Some librarians get extra training to become archivists. They work with historical information.

In the Community

Has a librarian helped you find the information you need? Librarians help many people. Students find books that help them with homework. Others want to find DVDs and learn how to use the Internet. Librarians are important workers in every community.

Some librarians help people online. Librarians answer questions through e-mails and in chat rooms. They also help people by phone.

A Day as a Librarian

Morning

Start work at 8:00 AM at the library.
Look in a journal or a catalog.
Choose books to buy for the library.

Late Morning

Answer questions by e-mail.
Listen to questions from a person.
Help the person find a book.

Afternoon

Teach a class about the Internet.
Read a story to children.
Show a person where the DVDs are kept.

Late Afternoon

Work at the help desk.
Show a person how to use a database.
Attend a librarians' union meeting.
End the day at 5:00 PM at the library.

Glossary

college—a school that a student goes to after high school.

computer programs—directions that make a computer work in a certain way.

databases—information that is sorted and stored on a computer.

information—facts about different things.

Internet—a system that connects computers to other computers.

library materials—the books, journals, magazines, newspapers, CDs, and DVDs that are in a library.

license—a government certificate that allows a person to do something.

union—a group that helps workers gain fair pay and safe working conditions.

volunteer—a person who gives their own time to work for a cause or an organization.

Web site—a place on the Internet that holds information about a subject or a place.

Did You Know?

The first known librarian was Gabriel Naudé. He was a Frenchman who lived in the 1600s. He wrote a book about how to start a library.

Laura Bush was the forty-third First Lady of the United States. She was also once a librarian and teacher in Texas.

On the Web

To learn more about librarians, visit ABDO Group online at **www.abdopublishing.com**. Web sites about librarians are featured on our Book Links page. These links are routinely monitored and updated to provide the most current information available.

Index